FINANC
FOR COLLEGE

RONALD W. JOHNSON
AND
MARC ROBINSON

DK

DORLING KINDERSLEY
London • New York • Sydney • Delhi • Paris • Munich • Johannesburg

A DORLING KINDERSLEY BOOK

Editors Ruth Strother, Stephanie Rubenstein
Design and Layout Hedayat Sandjari
Photography Anthony Nex
Project Editor Crystal A. Coble
Project Art Editor Mandy Earey
DTP Designer Jill Bunyan
Photo Research Mark Dennis, Sam Ruston
Indexing Rachel Rice
Editorial Director LaVonne Carlson
Design Director Tina Vaughan
Publisher Sean Moore

First American Edition, 2000
05 10 9 8 7 6 5 4 3 2

Published in the United States by
Dorling Kindersley Publishing, Inc.
375 Hudson Street,
New York, New York 10014
See our complete catalog at
www.dk.com

Packaged by Top Down Productions
Copyright © 2000
Dorling Kindersley Publishing, Inc.
Text copyright © 2000 Marc Robinson

Dorling Kindersley Publishing, Inc. offers special discounts
for bulk purchases for sales promotions or premiums.
Specific, large quantity needs can be met with special
editions, including personalized covers, excerpts of
existing guides, and corporate imprints. For more
information, contact Special Markets Dept., Dorling
Kindersley Publishing, Inc., 375 Hudson Street, NY, NY
10014; Fax: (800) 600-9098

Library of Congress Cataloging-in-Publication Data
Robinson, Marc, 1955-
  Financial aid for college / Marc Robinson and Ronald W. Johnson.
    p. cm. – (Essential finance)
  Includes index.
  ISBN 0-7894-6317-2
  1. Student aid–United States. 2. Education, Higher–United States–
Finance. I. Johnson, Ronald Wayne, 1942- II. Title. III. Series.

LB2337.4.R62 2000
37830'0973–dc21   00-031494

Reproduced by Colourscan, Singapore
Printed in China

CONTENTS

INTRODUCTION

An education is one of the most valuable resources anyone can have. Being able to pay for that education is the first step toward a successful future. Understanding how the financial aid process works is vital to making college affordable. An organized approach will make your time more efficient and your decisions more productive. As Financial Aid for College reveals, the process of finding money is not as complicated as many people are led to believe. This book is designed to give you instant access to the most important information without bogging you down in details. Inside you will see how to find out what college will cost, how much of your own money you will be expected to pay, options for saving and investing, ways to find free money and low-cost loans, and how to protect yourself from too much debt. You will also learn about the people, websites, and phone numbers that can make the entire experience easier for you.

5

WHAT WILL COLLEGE COST?

Don't let numbers intimidate you. Like buying a home or car, you can pay for college with some cash and finance the rest. Plus, there may be free money and subsidies to help.

YOUR GOAL IS THE COA

The Cost of Attendance (COA) is the cost of one year of college. Every school calculates its COA each year. Ask for it when considering whether to apply. Here are some averages to help you know what to expect.

WRONG GUESSES

According to a Gallup poll, many people think that college is more expensive than it is. The 13-21 year olds polled overestimated the average cost of public two- and four-year schools by more than 300% and private four-year schools by more than 33%.

COLLEGE COSTS 1999-2000

FOUR YEAR PRIVATE SCHOOLS		FOUR YEAR PUBLIC SCHOOLS	
1998-99	1999-2000	1998-99	1999-2000
$14,709	$15,380	$3,247	$3,356

TWO YEAR PRIVATE SCHOOLS		TWO YEAR PUBLIC SCHOOLS	
1998-99	1999-2000	1998-99	1999-2000
$6,940	$7,182	$1,554	$1,627

Note: Students attending out-of-state schools may have additional charges that increase tuition and fees beyond the averages. This year, tuition and fee charges for out-of-state students at public schools averaged $3,191 at two-year colleges and $5,350 at four-year colleges. The combined total averages for students facing additional charges was $4,818 for two-year schools and $8,706 for four-year schools.

EXPENSIVE MAY MEAN CHEAPER

Many private colleges have a lot of money to award and great flexibility in the ways they may award it. As a result, you might receive a financial aid package from an expensive school that will actually make it less expensive to attend than a school with a lower COA.

1 Don't rule out any school just because it seems too expensive.

WHAT STUDENTS ARE PAYING

TUITION RANGE	% OF TOTAL UNDERGRADUATE ENROLLMENT
$20,000 or more	4.3%
18,000-19,999	2.3
16,000-17,999	2.1
14,000-15,999	4.1
12,000-13,999	5.4
10,000-11,999	4.2
8,000-9,999	3.7
6,000-7,999	2.8
4,000-5,999	15.3
2,000-3,999	42.2
Less than $2,000	13.6
Total	100%

Note: The table shows the distribution of full-time undergraduates at 4-year colleges by tuition charged in 1996-1997. Figures include only those 1,601 public and private institutions that provided final or estimated expenses.

Source: The College Board

CLARIFY YOUR ESTIMATE

There are other costs you should take into account. For example, ask each school about options such as these:

- Is there room and board at different rates for different levels of service?
- Can you live off campus for less?
- Will there be special fees, such as for lab, athletics, insurance, computers, sororities/fraternities? If so, are there any options?
- How many years does the average student take to graduate? How much have costs increased in each of the last five years?

2 The numbers shown here are averages. Many schools will cost less.

HOW TO REACH YOUR GOAL

T hink of these categories as an overview of the financial aid landscape. Everything it takes to pay for college falls into one of the following four categories.

+

WHAT YOU CAN CONTRIBUTE

Expected Family Contribution (EFC). Every family applying for aid is expected to contribute a fair share of its own money each year. That share is called the EFC. It's sent to all the schools to which you've applied, and it's the official basis for determining financial aid.

Based on a formula. Your own EFC is based on a nationally standardized formula established by Congress. It analyzes your family's assets, income, and expenses, and the family profile, such as size and number of members in college. It then calculates how much your family is believed to be capable of paying.

THE FINANCIAL AID PACKAGE

Based solely on need. After reviewing the family's finances and EFC, the college's financial aid office decides how much aid they can offer each student accepted for admission. They draw on money from the school's own account, and from state and federal programs. You may receive financial aid in up to three forms:

- Grants and scholarships are free money you won't have to repay;
- Low-cost loans are money you will have to repay;
- Work-study programs provide money students earn to offset costs.

Reapply each year. You must reapply each year. Your financial aid package could change yearly, depending on the resources available to the school and any changes in your own financial status.

+  =

The Annual Cost of School

This is your goal: to meet the college's COA. By adding up the numbers you get from the first three columns, you hope to reach the cost in this column. The cost of a year's education varies, of course, from school to school. If you want to know a school's COA before applying, you can call the financial aid office or look on the school's website.

Decided by a set of rules. Each school has to determine its COA according to a nationally established set of rules. The following expenses are included in every school's COA:
- Tuition and fees;
- Room and board;
- Books and supplies;
- Travel to and from school;
- Some basic personal expenses.

The Unmet Need

If a financial aid package leaves a funding gap (which financial aid officers call an unmet need), you will have to find the remaining money elsewhere. Your main choices are:

Outside scholarships. Many states, companies, and organizations offer scholarships based on financial need, skill, or talent. Some are based on personal characteristics or affiliations such as religion, national origin, or a connection with a particular group;

Traditional loans. Students and parents can take loans from federal and state governments regardless of financial need. Private lenders also offer loans with special repayment plans;

Tuition assistance. Many employers offer tuition assistance programs to employees' families;

Loans based on assets. Homeowners may be able to borrow against their home equity. Some retirement plans and life insurance programs may also be tapped for education loans.

3 The COA appears on every financial aid award letter.

9

WHERE WILL YOU FIND THE MONEY?

There's a lot of money available to college-bound students, especially for those who have learned how to look. The people with money to give have their own goals and usually look to award students who will help further those goals. Once you grasp this concept, you can think about how to present yourself in the proper light and how to seek out compatible resources.

THE STUDENT

When seeking money, emphasize your:
- Skills and talents;
- Financial need;
- Personal qualities (ethnicity, sex, national origin, religion,etc.);
- Affiliations (employers, local and national organizations);
- Ability to earn, save, and invest money.

THE PARENTS

If possible, parents can contribute by:
- Using savings;
- Working part- or full-time;
- Securing a loan;
- Understanding the student's profile and helping to find scholarships and grants.

BANKS

Banks provide education loans in order to profit from the interest payments. Sometimes they use their own money. More often, they channel money that is provided by state and federal governments specifically for college loans. Government or private agencies usually guarantee repayment in case you *default* (fail to repay the loan). Ask the college's financial aid offices for a recommended list of lenders.

SCHOOLS

Colleges offer the money they have raised privately or received from government programs. Budgets are limited. Decisions are made with the school's interest at heart. For example, the school may want to boost the science department, raise its average test scores, find great basketball players, or add more ethnic diversity. Therefore, the school may offer financial aid to students who meet many of its enrollment goals, not simply to students with top grades.

FEDERAL AND STATE GOVERNMENTS

The federal government is the largest source of education funding. It funnels money to schools, banks, and directly to students for loans, grants, scholarships, and work-study programs.

States also offer aid to schools, banks, and students. By supporting their schools (public and private), they try to keep good citizens at home, draw in out-of-staters, and strengthen their economies.

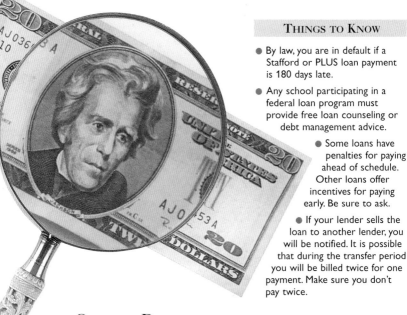

THINGS TO KNOW

- By law, you are in default if a Stafford or PLUS loan payment is 180 days late.

- Any school participating in a federal loan program must provide free loan counseling or debt management advice.

- Some loans have penalties for paying ahead of schedule. Other loans offer incentives for paying early. Be sure to ask.

- If your lender sells the loan to another lender, you will be notified. It is possible that during the transfer period you will be billed twice for one payment. Make sure you don't pay twice.

OTHER RESOURCES

The list of those who offer grants, scholarships, and other aid is vast, ranging from corporations and foundations to associations of all kinds. Employers also have become a major resource for assistance. Some want to fund students who can further a certain field of interest. Others want to help students in particular locations. Still others simply want to boost their organization's public image. Ask a guidance counselor or librarian how to uncover funding sources.

START INVESTING EARLY!

T*he first part of the money-raising equation is the portion you will have to pay from your own savings. Most people can't count on receiving grants or scholarships, so saving for college is a wise thing to do.*

SAVING VERSUS SPENDING

Even a little savings each month, therefore, can lead to a lot more money for college than you might think. Assume that you invest $100 a month in something that earns an average annual return of 8%. After five years, if you spend the profits, your savings will be $6,000. If you don't spend the profits, your savings will be $7,348. The gap widens considerably if you have 10, 15, or 20 years until you need the money. Over 20 years, the simple act of spending could cost you nearly $35,000. That's how much compounding accelerates earnings.

4 Compound growth is one of the most powerful and simplest ways to make money in investing.

MONEY'S ACCELERATED GROWTH

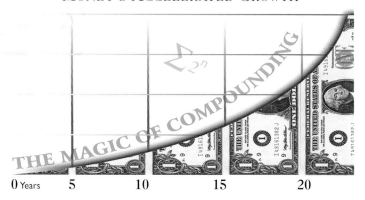

THE MAGIC OF COMPOUNDING

0 Years   5   10   15   20

5 For college, as with a car or a home, you can pay only a portion in cash (or maybe none at all).

SAVE MORE, PAY LESS

Some people think that building savings hurts their chances for aid, and therefore it isn't worth doing. Loans, however, are a large part of many financial aid packages. So the more money a family contributes, the less the student will be saddled with debt after graduation.

SAVINGS ADD UP

This table can help you understand how much you can accumulate over time even by saving small amounts each week. If you don't think you have enough time to accumulate much money before college, then consider starting now and using four years of additional growth to help repay loans after college.

Total value of account after:	If you save: $10/week	$12.50/week	$25/week	$50/week
2 years	$1,150	$1,438	$2,875	$5,751
3 years	$1,818	$2,272	$4,544	$9,087
4 years	$2,555	$3,194	$6,388	$12,775
5 years	$3,370	$4,213	$8,425	$16,850
10 years	$8,926	$11,158	$22,316	$44,632
15 years	$18,087	$22,609	$45,218	$90,437
20 years	$33,191	$41,489	$82,979	$165,956

Note: assumes a 10% return, which is a reasonable, but not an aggressive, projection.

6 Every year you save money can add a lot to the amount you will have at the end.

SOME BASIC INVESTMENTS

E ssentially, there are three main strategies for investing,
depending on how close you are to your goal. There are
also certain types of investments best suited to each strategy.

PROTECT MONEY: SHORT-TERM INVESTMENTS

These investments are designed to protect what you've earned and pay a little interest. They are good for people with five years or less before college. Beware of advice that treats them as long-term savings vehicles for college. Depending on how much you will pay to taxes and how much will be eroded by inflation, you typically won't earn much toward college. Both stocks and bonds have historically been better investments for the long-term.

Money market funds and savings accounts. You earn interest and invest for as short or as long as you wish. The interest is taxable. A bank money market fund or savings account is federally insured up to $100,000. Money market funds offered by mutual fund companies aren't federally insured.

Certificates of Deposit (CD). You buy CDs through financial institutions. The interest remains fixed for the time you own them. If interest rates rise while you own the CD, you won't benefit any further; but if they fall, you will be locked into a better rate than new CD buyers. There are penalties for withdrawing money early.

GROW MONEY: STOCKS

A share of stock gives you a share of ownership in the company that issued it. Your fortunes, therefore, rise and fall with the fortunes of the company. While the investment world divides stocks into many groups, you should understand at least these three.

Growth stocks. These are usually smaller companies that, because of their size or industry, have plenty of room to grow. Therefore, the price of a growth stock—which reflects the value of the company—also has plenty of room to rise. Be aware, though, that these stocks may be volatile (their prices could rise and fall unpredictably). Most experts say if you have at least 10 years until college, price volatility should not be a major concern.

Income stocks. These are usually companies with a record of strong, consistent profits. Their stock prices typically don't rise or fall dramatically, although there is certainly no rule saying they can't. The main attractions are the dividends they pay (a share of profits paid regularly to shareholders) and the opportunity for the price to rise.

Blue chips. These are the strongest companies in America, generally considered to be some of the safest stock investments. Investors with many years before college may also see these stocks' values rising significantly.

EARN A SET AMOUNT: BONDS

Bonds pay interest on a regular basis and typically are less sensitive than stocks to price swings.

Treasury bonds. By buying these bonds, you're lending money to the federal government—possibly the safest of investments since it's unlikely the government will declare bankruptcy and stop paying. You will owe federal income tax on the interest but, in most cases, no state or local income taxes.

Municipal bonds. Buying municipal bonds usually means lending money to help a state or local government fund projects such as construction and repairs. Generally, the interest is free of state taxes if you live in the state that issued the bond.

Corporate bonds. You can lend money to corporations. The interest earned is taxable. Corporations try to attract investors by offering to pay higher interest rates than could be earned from tax-free bonds. Whether you will earn more money from a corporate bond or a municipal bond may depend on your tax bracket.

> **7** Ask a tax or financial advisor for help with your specific situation.

15

INVESTING PEGGED TO COLLEGE YEARS

Y*ou can invest in some products that are timed to make money available just when the college years begin. Ask a tax or financial advisor for help with your specific situation.*

SAVINGS BONDS

Offered by the U.S. government, savings bonds are sold in denominations from $50 to $10,000. Generally, you pay half of the full value but you receive the full value at maturity (the day your original investment is returned). They may also provide a tax break.

ZERO COUPON BONDS

Zeroes don't pay interest each year. Instead, you buy them at a discount and receive full price at maturity. The difference between the discount price and the full price is your income. In effect, you receive the interest in one lump sum at the end of the loan instead of installments.

Why buys them? The discount lets you buy more bonds with less cash and know exactly how much you will earn by a certain date. People buy zero coupon bonds, therefore, with maturity dates coinciding with the first year of college so they receive all the interest just when it's needed.

Beware taxes. You may have to pay annual income taxes even though you receive no annual interest. Buying zero coupon bonds in a tax-advantaged account should avoid annual taxes. Buying tax-free zero coupon bonds will eliminate the tax issue altogether.

8 The interest from some EE Bonds and I Bonds may be tax-free if used for education.

KIDDIE TAX

Parents can take advantage of the kiddie tax, which takes taxable income over $1,200 and taxes it at the parents' rate until the child reaches age 14. At that point, income is taxed at the child's rate.

9 You can buy savings bonds online at www.savingsbonds.gov.

◀ TYPES OF ACCOUNTS
Some strategies require specific accounts, not types of investments, that give you special tax advantages to increase your savings.

CUSTODIAL ACCOUNT

Investments in these accounts hold assets in a child's name. In most states, all the money becomes available to the child at age 18 for whatever use the child wishes. In some states, the age may be 25.

CLIFFORD TRUST

These trusts let you transfer money to the child after age 14. A trustee is named to manage the money.

CRUMMEY TRUST

You can make tax-free gifts to children each year. Married couples: up to $20,000 per year; single parents: up to $10,000 per year. Income can remain in the trust for as long as you wish.

EDUCATION IRA

You can contribute up to $500 a year into this IRA for anyone under age 18. Contributions are nondeductible and eligibility is unaffected by any amounts contributed to regular IRAs. Money grows tax-free and can also be withdrawn tax-free.

Who isn't eligible? Eligibility phases out for donors with adjusted gross incomes (AGIs) between $150,000 and $160,000 (if filing jointly) and between $95,000 and $110,000 (if filing singly).

Eligible expenses. These include tuition, books, supplies, and room and board.

Eligible use. You can use the account to pay for the college expenses of any family member (even if not the person named on the account). All the money must be withdrawn by the time the person named on the account reaches age 30. Any earnings not used for education will be subject to income taxation and a 10% penalty.

Note. If your income exceeds the limits for Education IRA investing, you can make a $500 gift per year to your child, who then opens an account in his/her name. Grandparents may also contribute for a grandchild.

 10 A trust is an account, not an investment.

THE FINANCIAL AID PACKAGE

The second part of the money-raising equation
is the financial aid package that may be offered by
a school that accepts you for enrollment.

YOUR EFC IS THE KEY

*T*he Expected Family Contribution (EFC) is the minimum amount
your family will be expected to contribute toward college. It's based
on the nationally standardized formula described here. Most of all, the EFC
determines the types and amounts of aid you are eligible to receive.

Some websites
have EFC
calculators to help
you know what to
expect to pay.

EXCLUSIONS

Home equity and retirement
plans are excluded from total
income and assets, recognizing
that families shouldn't have to
put these assets in jeopardy.

TOTAL INCOME AND ASSETS

To cover the annual cost of college you are expected to contribute:

Students. Up to 35% of personal assets and 50% of income;

Parents. Up to 5.6% of assets and a portion of available income.

FAMILY PROFILE

The income included in the formula is reduced based on:

Size of the family. Larger families need to keep more money to support themselves;

Family members in college. Sending two or more at the same time is a greater burden;

Parents' ages. The older you get, the closer you will be to needing money for retirement.

CERTAIN EXPENSES

Other reductions based on:

- The total Social Security and income taxes you will have to pay;
- Some health expenses (recognizing that healthcare shouldn't be considered a discretionary expense).

INCOME ALLOWANCE

The final figure at the end of the calculation, shows how much of your family's assets will be exempt from the EFC calculation.

OPEN IT ▶

Experts say that everyone should fill out FAFSA to open every aid resource possible.

THE EFC

The result is the amount you will be expected to contribute to a year of school. This amount won't be covered by federal, state, or school financial aid.

FREE MONEY
AKA "GIFT AID"

T*he best way to finance an education is with someone else's money that you won't be asked to repay. The Pell Grant is the largest federal need-based grant program. Pell Grant money is the first layer of a financial aid package to be awarded to those most in financial need (based on their EFC).*

FEDERAL PELL GRANT

Maximum per student: $400 to $3,300 per year. This grant from the federal government is the largest need-based program, offered directly to students demonstrating "exceptional need" (an EFC of $2,926 or less). The amount of aid is based on:

- The Cost of Attendance (COA) at the college of your choice;
- Your family's financial need;
- The length of the college program (two-and four-year);
- Whether you will be a part- or full-time student.

HOW YOU ARE PAID

A school must notify you in writing about the amount of your Pell Grant and/or SEOG and how it will be paid. It is the school's choice to:

- Pay you directly by check;
- Credit your school account;
- Combine a payment and credit.

THINGS TO KNOW

- Recipients must file a Statement of Educational Purpose, stating that all of the funds will be used for only educational purposes.

- Students may receive only one Pell Grant per year and must reapply each year.

- The U.S. Department of Education guarantees that each participating school will receive enough money to pay the federal Pell Grants of its eligible students. There's no guarantee every eligible student will be able to receive a federal SEOG. Students at each school are paid based on the availability of funds at that school.

> **12** The government can change the money limits on Pell Grants each year.

THE SEOG

Maximum per student: $4,000 per year. The federal government gives participating colleges a fixed amount of money each year for this program (check to see whether the colleges you're interested in participate). Each school then distributes the money as part of its own aid package. SEOG money is offered to low-income students and those with the most financial need. In most cases, you must first qualify for a federal Pell Grant to be eligible for the SEOG.

> **13** A school cannot refuse to give you Pell Grant money simply because you are enrolled less than half-time.

TO BE ELIGIBLE

You must:
- Demonstrate financial need;
- Have a high school diploma or GED;
- Be a U.S. citizen, or eligible non-citizen;
- Be enrolled in or accepted to a participating program that is approved by the U.S. Department of Education;
- Have a valid Social Security number;
- Make satisfactory academic progress;
- Have complied with U.S. Selective Service registration requirements;
- Not be in default on a student loan or owe a refund on another grant;
- Sign an Anti Drug Abuse Act Certification.

Part-time students may be eligible.

MORE FREE MONEY

F *ederal and state governments offer another kind of subsidized loan and work-study program to those who meet the financial need requirements (based on their EFC score). These programs are offered by the federal government regardless of your home state, but programs can vary from state to state.*

SCHOLARSHIPS

Scholarships provide money mainly for tuition payments. Typically, they are awarded based on academic merit, a talent, or a skill. Some, however, are based on financial need.

Why they are awarded. Many go to students who seem likely to succeed or are inclined to advance the cause of the community, organization, or industry. That's why many scholarships are awarded simply because a student fits a certain profile such as gender, ethnicity, religion, or even career choice.

Some guidelines. There's no limit to the number of scholarships you can receive. Most are one-year awards, beginning July 1 and ending June 30 the following year. Some are renewable, but many require that you reapply each year with no guarantee of renewal.

While many scholarships are awarded without condition, some come with strings attached. Students must fulfill certain obligations (usually involving academics or sports) or risk having the money reconsidered as a loan that must be repaid.

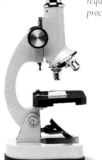

▲ SPECIAL ATHLETIC RULES

Student athletes can visit www.ncaa.org/eligibility/cbsa or call the NCAA at 317-917-6222 for information on recruiting rules, GPA and testing requirements, and registration procedures.

WEB RESEARCH

There are many legitimate online resources for scholarship searches. You might visit www.fastweb.com to start. Ask your guidance counselor for other suggestions.

EMPLOYEE TUITION BENEFITS

Many companies offer to pay part of the tuition for children of employees. Most colleges will treat this aid as an outside scholarship. Check with your company's human resources department.

MAKE MUSIC ▶
Even if artistic scholarships typically are not abundant, check at each school. Some receive gifts from alumni specifically for arts scholarships.

SCAM ALERT

The Federal Trade Commission (FTC) has a program to help you spot scams and rip-offs. It's called Project ScholarScam. For a consumer education kit, contact the FTC in Washington, D.C., or email consumerline@ftc.gov. A request for payment is always the first warning sign, because there are many free ways to locate scholarships.

CAN YOU HANDLE IT?

Research has shown that students who work up to 20 hours per week do at least as well academically as those who don't work.

---

14 Legitimate search firms never guarantee they will find you a grant or scholarship.

GOVERNMENT SUBSIDIZED WORK:
FEDERAL WORK-STUDY PROGRAM

Federal work-study is not quite free money but at least it's money you won't have to repay. Work is awarded as part of a financial aid package, so the college decides who receives the jobs (you will see it in the award letter).

WAGES
At least minimum wage.

TYPICAL WORK WEEK
10-20 hours.

ELIGIBILITY
Based on financial need as measured by the EFC.

EXPECTED INCOME
$1,000-$2,000/yr. for 10-20 hours per week of work. Actual amounts vary every year depending upon the allocation to the college, your class schedule, course load, and financial need.

WORK PROFILE
Typically, jobs are on campus, but there could be off-campus work.

OTHER AID
BASED ON NEED

There are three federally subsidized loan programs. Most schools participate in at least one.

FEDERAL PERKINS LOAN

These loans are awarded by the college to students who are most in need. Repayment is postponed until after graduation (or earlier, if the student leaves school). The amount awarded depends on the funds available at the college (up to $3,000 per year at the lowest rate of any student loan).

- The maximum combined loan amount is $15,000;
- The interest rate is fixed at 5%;
- Payments begin nine months after leaving school, unless the student enters the military, Peace Corps, or another comparable, approved organization;
- You may take up to 10 years to repay in full.

15

The federal government can pay the interest on subsidized loans while the student is in school.

MASTER PROMISSORY NOTE

The Stafford Loan Master Promissory Note is a promise that you will live up to all the terms and conditions of your loan agreements. If the school you attend uses this note to cover all of your loans, you will only have to complete it the first time you borrow. It's a binding contract, so be sure to read it carefully before signing.

STAFFORD LOAN (FFEL)

Available for freshmen: up to $2,625 per year.
For sophomores: up to $3,500 per year.
For juniors and seniors: up to $5,500 per year.

- Maximum combined is $23,000;
- Maximum interest rate is 8.25%;
- Payments begin six months after leaving school;
- Full repayment: up to 10 years.

The repayment plan is worked out between the lender and borrower. It may be postponed based on at least half-time study, approved graduate school study, or economic hardship.

16 To qualify, for federal loans, a student must be enrolled in school at least half-time.

THINGS TO KNOW

● The FFEL is more commonly called the Stafford Loan.

● FFEL loans are made by commercial lenders such as banks, credit unions or savings and loan associations (you will have a choice of lender). The federal government pays the interest while the student is in school. The loans are insured by a guaranty agency and are reinsured by the government.

● A school may offer either the Stafford or the Direct Loan, but not both.

FEDERAL FORD DIRECT LOAN

Often referred to as simply the Direct Loan, this loan has the same terms as the Stafford Loan. The main difference is, the government gives the money directly to the school, which in turn applies it to the bill owed by the student. The student then repays the

 17 The Master Promissory Note is a new tool to make applying for loans easier.

THE PROCESS OF BORROWING

1) Get an application form from the school or lender;

2) Fill it out (including the promissory note) and return it to the school's financial aid office;

3) If you are eligible, the school sends your application to the lender;

4) The lender sends it to a guaranty agency;

5) The guaranty agency reviews it and determines if the loan will be guaranteed;

6) If approved, you receive a promissory note and/or loan disclosure statement and a statement of rights and responsibilities;

7) The student signs the promissory note and the lender issues a check;

8) Fees of 4% are deducted from the loan;

9) The money is sent directly to the school, usually in two installments: at the start of each semester and 30 days after classes begin.

THE UNMET NEED

The last part of your money-raising equation involves finding money you may still need, after financial aid, to cover the cost of attendance.

STATE AID

E *very state awards aid based on need. Many also have merit-based scholarships. Some state aid may be awarded by the college in its financial aid package. If not, state aid can be an additional resource to fill any unmet need. Call your state's educational agency for information.*

18
Remember the filing deadlines! Missing them can cost you money.

WORK-STUDY

Some states offer their own version of the federal work-study program. Check with your state guaranty agency. A job could be during school or in the summer. Some work-study programs may also help you advance your on-the-job training into a full-time position after school.

TUITION RECIPROCITY

At least 14 states allow students from other states to pay the reduced tuition reserved for residents of that state.

PREPAID TUITION PLANS

These state-run programs let parents pay for college in the future at today's prices. Parents contribute regularly to a fund for each child they enroll, and that fund is used for tuition when the child goes to college. Parents must sign a contract and enroll in the state-sponsored program. Some plans are only for residents. Others are more flexible. Prepaying may protect your money from inflation and other cost increases, but it may also lock your child into a school that may turn out to be inappropriate for him/her.

COMMON APPLICATION ERRORS

Some states require you to file a GPA Verification Form when applying for state aid. Here are the three most common errors students make, according to the State of California:

- The school verification entry is left blank. In 1998-1999, the state received over 2,500 forms without school certifications;
- There is no Social Security number or an incorrect number. Without this, the form can't be matched with your FAFSA (see page 52);
- There is no financial aid administrator signature (or the signature section was completed by the student). The student's GPA can't be verfied without the administrator's signature.

LOAN FORGIVENESS

Many states will let you end your loan payments permanently if you enter certain professions they're trying to develop in-state. Examples include jobs in education and healthcare.

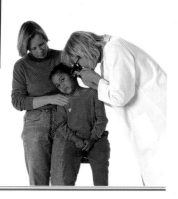

SPECIAL CAREER PROGRAMS

Some states offer grants and subsidized loans. Some states even have programs where they will assume some of your loan debt in return for public service in a field of interest, such as public health, for a certain number of years.

TAX CREDITS

T he easiest way to bridge some or all of the gap is to use the tax breaks offered by the federal government to stimulate higher education.

HOPE SCHOLARSHIP

"Scholarship" is a misleading name. This is actually a tax credit for:

- Up to $1,500 a year per eligible student;
- No more than two tax years.

How it works. You claim up to 100% of the first $1,000 of eligible expenses and 50% of the next $1,000 (which makes the maximum of $1,500). You don't get a refund if the credit is larger than the tax you owe.

How you get it. The IRS requires schools to give students a form that describes their eligible expenses, and to assist the student in filing for the credit.

Eligibility rules. A student must:

- Be enrolled at least half-time in an eligible program at an eligible school;
- Be a freshman or sophomore in college;
- Not have been convicted of a felony drug offense before the end of the tax year in which the school year ends.

Who uses the credit. To be eligible, you must:

- File a tax return;
- Owe taxes (not be receiving a refund);
- Claim the student as your dependent on the tax return (unless the student is you or your spouse);
- Owe less in taxes than the maximum credit available to you under the Hope Scholarship.

NO LIMIT ▶
There's no total dollar limit per family for the education tax credits. If you have three kids in college, you could potentially have three $1,500 tax credits.

19

You can't take a tax credit in any year you take a withdrawal from an education IRA.

MORE CREDIT

A family can claim both of these tax credits and exclusions from gross income for certain distributions from qualified state tuition programs and education IRAs as long as:

- The family doesn't exceed the Lifetime Learning Tax Credit;
- The same student isn't used as the basis for each benefit.

DEDUCTION VS. CREDIT

A tax deduction reduces the taxable income you have. A tax credit is more powerful. The amount is subtracted directly from the tax you owe.

LIFETIME LEARNING TAX CREDIT

This is a tax credit for:
- Up to $1,000 a year (until Jan. 1, 2003, then $2,000 per year after that);
- Each family (not each student);
- An unlimited number of years.

How it works. You claim 20% of up to $5,000 of paid eligible expenses (20% of $10,000 after Jan.1, 2003). There's no refund if the credit is larger than the amount of tax you owe.

How you get it. The IRS requires schools to give students a form that describes their eligible expenses, and to assist the student in filing for the credit.

Eligibility rules. A student must:
- Be enrolled at least half-time in an eligible program at an eligible school;
- Be a freshman or sophomore in college;
- Not have been convicted of a felony drug offense before the end of the tax year in which the school year ends.

Who uses the credit. To be eligible to use the credit, you must:
- File a tax return;
- Owe taxes (not be receiving a refund);
- Claim the student as your dependent on the tax return (unless the student is you or your spouse).

FULL AND PARTIAL CREDIT

You're eligible for full credit if your adjusted gross income (AGI) is:
- $40,000 or less if filing singly;
- $80,000 or less if filing jointly.

You're eligible for partial Hope Scholarship credit if your AGI is:
- $50,000 or less if filing singly;
- $100,000 or less if filing jointly.

The amount of your Lifetime Learning credit is gradually reduced between $40,000-$50,000; $80,000-$100,000 if filing jointly.

LOAN INTEREST DEDUCTION

You can deduct interest on education loans—up to $2,500. Only the interest you're required to pay during the first five years of the loan is deductible. The deduction is phased out for AGIs between $60,000 and $75,000 if filing jointly and $40,000 and $55,000 if filing singly. If you are over the limit, you may be able to borrow in the student's name and receive the deduction, as long as the student isn't claimed as your dependent.

SPECIAL PROGRAMS

If you fall into one of the categories listed below, you may be eligible for one of the many resources for scholarships, grants, tuition waivers, and other awards. Ask your high school guidance counselor, as well as representatives of the colleges you're considering.

VETERANS BENEFITS

Current personnel and veterans discharged from active duty within the past 10 years may be eligible for benefits under one of many VA educational programs. Dependents of deceased or disabled veterans from any service era may also be eligible for benefits and/or fee waivers. Consult a Veterans Affairs counselor to check eligibility.

Where to apply. Applications for all educational VA benefits can be obtained from the Department of Veterans Affairs or the school's Veterans Affairs/Student Financial Services office and must be submitted to the Veterans Affairs office for official certification.

20 Churches are an excellent resource for learning about financial aid based on minority status.

WOMEN'S PROGRAMS

There are many programs designed specifically for women, including working women and mothers. Programs come from the federal and state levels as well as from colleges and private sources. Contact as many government and private entities geared to women as you can. A fast way to start is to type "financial aid for women" into Internet search engines.

PEOPLE WITH DISABILITIES

Most state and local organizations will know what financial aid programs are available for your specific situation, or they will know where to send you for that information. Financial aid officers and guidance counselors may also know.

Financial aid. Every state has an agency for job training (almost always with a name that includes "rehabilitation services"). They all offer assistance with tuition and other college expenses. If you're looking for work while in school, contact the Handicapped Information Resources for Employment, 95 Chestnut Ridge Road, Montvale, New Jersey, 07645.

Scholarships. The National Federation of the Blind, in Grinnell, Iowa, offers scholarships to legally blind students. The American Foundation for the Blind, in New York City, offers scholarships to the blind. The Alexander Graham Bell Association for the Deaf, in Washington, D.C., offers scholarships to prelingually deaf students.

22 Inform financial aid officers of handicap-related expenses so they can be considered when calculating financial need.

THINGS TO KNOW

- The law requires that anyone receiving assistance from a rehabilitation agency also apply for federal financial aid (using FAFSA, see page 52).
- Disabled people should coordinate efforts between the school's financial aid officer and the agency administrator.
- Schools must meet their disabled students needs or risk losing federal financial aid funds.

21 Many schools offer day care facilities. Some offer financial aid to cover the cost.

MINORITY STATUS

For minorities, aid is available through many programs from the federal government, states, and even the colleges themselves. Many foundations, as well as private and religious groups, also offer aid.

Eligibility. Minority status includes:
- African Americans;
- Latinos;
- Native Americans.

A fast way to get started is to type "financial aid for minorities" into Internet search engines.

WORK FOR MONEY

You can save tuition costs by working before, during, or after college. If your course load allows it, you might work 10-20 hours a week and earn $1,000-$2,000 or more a year. Work programs can be career related, giving you a jump on post-graduation plans (overlapping information below means you can work in either period).

BEFORE COLLEGE

WORK FOR COLLEGE CREDIT

Some schools give you class credits for work experience. This lets you make money and lower the amount of time and number of credits you will need to graduate.

INTERNSHIPS AND FELLOWSHIPS

Work may be available in federal government positions. High school students can ask guidance counselors about the Junior Fellowship Program. College students can ask at the financial aid office.

DURING COLLEGE

IN-SCHOOL JOB PLACEMENT

Every school has a placement office that helps students find work on and off campus. Positions aren't based on need. It's possible that a job during school can lead to a permanent position after school.

AFTER COLLEGE

SAVE A LOT OF LOAN DEBT

Working while in school can be a physical and emotional strain but can help you avoid having to carry big loans for many years. Consider that borrowing $8,000 could cost $12,000, including interest, by the time it's repaid, so earning $8,000 ($2,000 per year) could actually save you $12,000.

THINGS TO KNOW

Work affects your EFC. Half of your after-tax income over $2,200 will be added to your EFC. Remember to include this in your calculations.

COOPERATIVE EDUCATION

These programs let you alternate working full-time and going to school full-time. Many federal and corporate jobs are included.

Requirements: Jobs are open to anyone. They aren't based on need.
Payment: Salaries vary based on on the work you do.

DORM BOSS

You can apply for a position as a resident advisor in exchange for reductions in room and board costs. You live in the dorms with younger students and perform the roles asked of you by the school.

NATIONAL AND COMMUNITY SERVICE PROGRAM

This program is federally funded, but it is run by schools and outside organizations. Work is available during or after college to pay for tuition or repay loans.
Requirements: 1,700 hours (about 42 weeks) a year for two years.
Payment: $4,725 per year., plus $7,400 per year in living expenses.

GET HELP FROM THE MILITARY

If you're willing to trade a few years of your life in the military, the armed forces may give you money toward tuition. Here are three choices.

GO TO MILITARY SCHOOL

Service academies are four-year colleges that serve the branches of the armed forces. Their purpose is to educate and train students for careers as military officers. They offer a standard core of courses found at other colleges, plus courses in military training. You graduate with a four-year degree, but that's where the similarity with other colleges ends. For example, other than a one-time fee of under $2,000 (for a uniform, computer, and books), your education is free, and you earn a salary each year you're in school.

Admission standards and requirements are among the most competitive in the country. You must be near the top of your high school class, score high on SATs, pass a medical exam and fitness test, and except for the Coast Guard Academy, be nominated for admission by a member of Congress (each member of Congress may have only five nominees enrolled at service academies at any one time).

Life in an academy means a regimented daily schedule, attending classes in uniform, and participating in training exercises. In addition, you can't be married, pregnant, or have a legal obligation to support a child. Finally, upon graduation, you must serve a minimum of five years in active duty.

THREE MAIN CHOICES

All branches of the military offer training in various technical and vocational areas, and military enrollees can often obtain college credit for some of this training. The three main military academies are:

- U.S. Military Academy, located in West Point, New York;
- U.S. Naval Academy, located in Annapolis, Maryland;
- U.S. Air Force Academy, located in Colorado Springs, Colorado.

SERVE, THEN GO TO SCHOOL

The GI Bill is a program designed for people who choose to enlist in one of the branches of the armed forces first and pursue a college degree later. As military personnel, you can participate in the program by paying a $100 monthly fee for a year.

The money goes into the GI Bill fund and makes you eligible for educational benefits you can use either during or after your military service.

To qualify, you must serve at least three continuous years of active duty or two years of active duty followed by four years in the reserves. To be eligible, you must have a high school diploma and leave the military with an honorable discharge.

TRAIN WHILE IN SCHOOL

The Reserve Officers Training Corps (ROTC) offers a scholarship program that lets you go to college full-time and participate in a part-time or summer officer training program.

ROTC scholarships offer recipients free tuition, fees, and books for up to four years of school in exchange for up to four years of active duty following graduation. You also receive a salary during the last two years of school, a travel allowance, paid summer training, and free flights aboard military aircraft (when space is available).

You can apply for a scholarship at a military recruiting office during your high school junior or senior year. Competition is strong, but even if you don't receive a scholarship, you may enroll in an ROTC program (without tuition benefits) and reapply for a scholarship the following year.

You must be a U.S. citizen, a high school graduate, between the ages of 17 and 21, and pursuing an approved degree program. If you receive a scholarship, you must make "satisfactory academic progress" in order to keep it.

WHO TO CALL

For more information, contact your local armed forces recruiting office at 800-USA-ROTC or try www.armyrotc.com.

CREATIVE WAYS TO LOWER COSTS

*R*aising money is the most obvious way to pay for college. But another way is to lower costs, and there are many ways to do it. Here are some common alternatives to raising money to pay for college.

DEFERRED ENROLLMENT PLANS

Many colleges will accept you for admission in the future—maybe in a year or two. So, instead of attending classes in the upcoming term, you can work full-time to earn money toward a goal, not a dream.

LIVING AT HOME

This is an obvious but powerful savings option. It saves room and board (although it may not save commuting costs). Even if you go away from home, off-campus living with a roommate may save money.

TWO YEARS THEN TRANSFER

Many students live at home while attending a two-year community college for basic level courses and then transfer to a four-year school for their final two years. Be sure the community college courses are transferable to the four-year school you're planning to attend, otherwise you will be stuck retaking courses—at an even greater expense.

CO-OP EDUCATION

Over a thousand colleges let you alternate semesters of schooling and full-time work in a field related to your major (it's most common in the engineering and business fields). A co-op degree usually takes about five years. When you're done, you will have a body of work experience to present to potential employers.

SPECIAL ACADEMIC EXAMS

Students can earn college credits for basic courses before they even get to college. They do this by taking courses or tests designated as either Advanced Placement (AP), or College Level Exam Program (CLEP) courses. This saves money by cutting down the required college course load. But before enrolling in a course or test, be sure the colleges you may attend accept it.

ACCELERATED PROGRAMS

You can finish college in three years instead of four if the school's academic advisors give their approval. You will be out of school ahead of schedule and save a year's expenses. It will require a heavier course load each semester and no summer breaks, so this option may not be for everyone.

INDEPENDENT STUDENT STATUS

Students who meet the criteria can qualify for financial aid based on their financial status, instead of their parents' status. This can mean a lot more money from the various resources.

Students who will be at least 24 years old in their freshman year are considered independent. Younger students will be considered independent if they are:
- An armed forces veteran;
- An orphan or ward of the state;
- A student with legal dependents other than a spouse;
- A married person.

BORROWING FOR THE REST

The last alternative is to borrow whatever else you need.
Loans add to the expense of college, but they're a fact of life
for a large portion of the college-going population.

TAP INTO YOUR ASSETS

*You may not have to look any further
than your own resources. Schools that
ask for the FAFSA (see page 52) don't
include any of the assets here in their
financial need analysis. Therefore, you
may be able to receive a larger aid
package and also be able to borrow from
your family's assets to cover the unmet
need. Talk to a financial advisor.*

23 Term insurance
policies do not
have cash values
for borrowing.

LIFE INSURANCE

You may be able to borrow against the cash
value of your policy. Some policies invest your
premiums in tax-deferred accounts that tend to
grow your money faster than taxable accounts,
which can mean more money to use for college.
One benefit is that you can borrow from a policy
to pay for college without being taxed.

HOME EQUITY

Homeowners may be able to borrow money based on the amount of equity in their home. Equity is the home's current value minus the loan amount still owed.

Interest may be tax deductible. You may be told that home equity loans give you the added advantage of being tax deductible. That's not always true. Consult a financial or tax advisor about your specific situation.

Be aware. You may pay a significant amount in fees for the loan. In addition, the lender's processing could take a month or more—even if the lender promises you a quick turnaround. Most of all, you're putting your home at risk if you find yourself unable to make the payments.

RETIREMENT SAVINGS

You're allowed to borrow from an IRA or Keogh for educational purposes. Whether you can borrow from a 401(k) depends on your company's plan rules.

Repay with interest. You repay these loans with interest to your retirement plan, so in effect you pay yourself a fee for borrowing the money. That may seem like a win-win situation, but consider that money withdrawn means that there is less money invested to keep growing. That tends to cut down on potential earnings over the long run.

MORTGAGE REFINANCING

If your kids are young and you have many years before facing tuition bills, consider refinancing your mortgage from 30 years down to 15 years. You will have larger payments now, but by the time your kids go to college, your house may be mostly or fully paid off and you will have much more equity for an equity loan if you need it. In addition, you may be able to face tuition payments without the added burden of mortgage payments.

24 Be sure that it's a better financial decision to borrow from your 401(k) than from your home.

UNSUBSIDIZED LOANS

T*he federal government sponsors a number of unsubsidized loan programs open to anyone, regardless of financial need. The terms are more favorable than personal loans and many home equity loans. In fact, the main difference between these unsubsidized loans and their subsidized counterparts is that you must be creditworthy to borrow because the loans are not government guaranteed.*

FOR PARENTS

Parents can borrow money under one of two federal PLUS Loan programs. There are the FFEL PLUS and the Direct PLUS. **Loans.** Under the Direct PLUS Loan, the government sends the money directly to the school in installments. Under the FFEL PLUS Loan, you pay an approved financial institution, such as a bank. Ask the financial aid office for a list.

How to apply. Applications are available from a school's financial aid office. The FFEL PLUS application goes to the school, who passes it on to the lender.

Amounts. You can borrow up to the amount of your unmet need.

Cost. Rates are adjustable but go no higher than 9%. Additional fees can run up to 4% of the loan amount.

Terms. You have up to 10 years to repay. There is no grace period. Payments begin 60 days after the last loan amount is paid to the school.

Eligibility. You need a good credit record and must show the ability to repay what you owe.

25 You can apply for an unsubsidized loan regardless of financial need. Most schools do not require a FAFSA.

CHOOSE TO PAY INTEREST

In an unsubsidized loan (not based on need), you will be charged interest from the start of the loan. If you are permitted to defer payments, the interest will be capitalized (added to the amount you owe, so you will be paying interest on the interest). You may also be able to take a tax deduction on the interest during the first sixty months of the loan, which will save even more money.

FOR STUDENTS

Students can borrow money under the Unsubsidized Stafford Loan program. These loans are offered only to students who have filled out the FAFSA (see page 52). Schools provide a list of approved lenders. The lender you choose will pay the school directly and manage the loan.

Amount. You can borrow up to the full amount that fills your unmet need.

Cost. Rates are adjustable but can go no higher than 8.25%. Additional fees can run up to 4% of the loan amount. There may also be an insurance premium of up to 1%.

Terms. You have up to 10 years to repay.

Eligibility. Everyone is eligible.

Timing. The loan amount for first-year students is sent to the school 30 days after the first day of enrollment.

Payment options. There are two main options to choose from:

- Begin paying interest immediately. Payments on the principal portion will begin after you graduate;
- Elect to postpone all payments until graduation and have the interest payments that accumulate during the school years tacked onto your payments.

26 All funds from PLUS loans must be used to pay for education.

THINGS TO KNOW

- The federal government supplies lenders with money to distribute so that more loans can be made.

- The Department of Education is the Direct PLUS lender. To find a lender for a FFEL PLUS Loan, call the Federal Student Aid Information Center's toll-free number: 800-4FEDAID.

- Many reputable, private companies offer education loans. Competing for business, they often create new programs and adjust existing ones to accommodate a variety of borrowers' changing needs.

◀ LOAN ALTERNATIVE

Dependent students whose parents don't qualify for a PLUS loan can still apply for an unsubsidized Stafford Loan. Ask the college financial aid office for more information.

Private Loans

M*any lending institutions such as banks, credit unions, and student loan companies offer payment plans and loans up to the full amount you will need to fill the gap. Many college financial aid offices are willing to suggest reliable sources for loans.*

Loan amount. Some require you to borrow at least $1,500; others, at least $2,000. Most allow you to borrow up to the full tuition cost minus any financial aid you receive.

Rates. Rates are typically competitive with federal loan programs. Most rates are adjustable; they can go up or down monthly, quarterly, or annually.

Cost. Additional fees can range from a 5% guarantee fee, which the lender holds as a reserve in case you don't make payments (and may be refundable), up to 7% in origination fees (for getting the loan up and running).

Terms. Some programs require interest payments to begin immediately. Others allow payments to be postponed until after graduation. Still others allow for principal and interest payments to begin immediately in exchange for a lower interest rate. The length can vary greatly, from 4 years to 25 years.

Eligibility. You need to be creditworthy and show the ability to repay. Lenders will review your income, assets, and history of repaying debts. If you don't have much of a credit record, they may ask someone to co-sign the loan with you and guarantee the payments. Some programs also require the student to attend a federally eligible college. Check with the financial aid office.

TUITION PAYMENT PLANS

M*any colleges offer tuition payment plans where you can spread payments evenly over a number of months. Payments begin in the summer before freshman year. This allows the company offering the service to earn interest (its profit) on your money before it has to pay the college.*

Amount. *Most companies will allow you to enter into a plan covering the full amount of tuition.*

No credit check. *Since a payment plan is not a loan, there is no credit check and no interest payments.*

Cost. *There is no interest charge because it isn't a loan. However, the plan must be endorsed by the college because tuition payment plans are operated by private companies. Ask the financial aid office for a reference. There is an annual fee, usually less than $100.*

Terms. *Depending on the school's own policies, the payments are spread out over a 10-month year, or a five-month semester. You can apply money from a loan to the plan or use your own money.*

Eligibility. *These plans are typically open to anyone who pays tuition, regardless of financial need. You do not have to qualify for financial aid or have filled out FAFSA. Tuition payment plans are good for people who don't want to use all of their available cash at once, or need to stretch their limited resources as far as possible.*

UNDERSTAND YOUR LOAN

W*hile student loans are the most common type of financial aid, they're not to be taken lightly. Repayment becomes an ongoing responsibility whether or not you graduate, get a job, build a career, or start a family. Depending on the repayment terms, a loan could take 20 years or longer to repay.*

KNOW THE TERMS

If you repay your loans faithfully, you will build a good credit record that will help you rent or buy a home, buy a car, get credit cards, or succeed in a host of other situations. Failure to repay faithfully will limit these same opportunities. Knowing what you're agreeing to, therefore, is vital to your future financial health.

Principal and interest. The *principal* is the amount you borrow. The *interest* is the cost of the loan (the lender's fee). Your loan payments will usually include some principal and some interest.

Amount. Know how much your monthly payment will be. In the early years of most loans, the bulk of each payment goes to pay the interest while a small portion begins to repay what you borrowed. As the years progress, the proportions gradually shift, so that by the end, most of each payment goes to pay the principal and a small part goes toward the interest.

Repayment schedule. Know how long you will have to repay the entire loan, the date of the first payment, the day of the month each payment is due, and the date of the last payment.

27 The terms you accept can affect your borrowing power for many years to come.

28 Over time, more of each payment will go to pay off the loan and less will go to pay the lender's interest.

BORROWING HAS INCREASED

A 1997 study by the Institute for Higher Education Policy found that on average, parents borrowed $14,000 to pay for college during the 1997-98 school year, compared to $9,000 during the 1992-93 school year.

GAIN SOME INSIGHT

You might gain some insight into your borrowing future by looking at the schools you're considering. Ask the admissions officer:

- What percentage of students graduate?
- What percentage of students get jobs within six months of graduating?
- What is the loan default rate? This is the percentage of students who took out student loans but didn't repay them. A high rate may indicate that many students never completed school or were unable to make enough money after graduating. Colleges with consistently high default rates may be barred from student loan programs. Students at these schools may be ineligible for federal loans.

KNOW THE BREAKS

Since students aren't expected to make a lot of money until they're out of school for a while, loans are often structured with manageable repayment terms.

Grace period. Some loans require students to begin payments immediately. Others provide a grace period that allows students to begin payments either six or nine months after leaving school. If the loan is subsidized, the government pays the interest while the student is in school and during the grace period. If the loan is unsubsidized, the student is responsible for all of the interest.

Deferment. Students may be able to get a lender to postpone repayment for up to three years. To qualify, the student must usually be:

- On active duty in the military;
- A full-time volunteer in an approved program;
- In economic hardship;
- Enrolled in a participating graduate or professional program.

Cancellation. Students may be able to cancel a loan if they become disabled. Going into bankruptcy, however, probably won't release the obligation.

More to Understand

H*ere's more information to help guide your decision making process.*

Default

You default when you fail to repay a loan according to the terms agreed to when you signed the promissory note. Default also may result from failure to submit requests for deferment or cancellation on time. If you default, your school, the lender or agency that holds your loan, the state, and the federal government may all take action to recover the money, including notifying national credit bureaus of your default. This may affect your credit rating for a long time. For example, you may find it very difficult to borrow from a bank to buy a car, a house, or other large purchases.

In addition, the lender or agency holding your loan may ask your employer to deduct payments from your paycheck. You may also be liable for expenses incurred in collecting the loan. If you decide to return to school, you're not entitled to receive any more federal student aid or any of the deferments listed in the Loan Deferment Summary. The U.S. Department of Education may ask the U.S. Internal Revenue Service to withhold your income tax refund, so the amount of your refund can be applied toward the amount you owe.

Repayment Choices for FFEL Loans

There are four ways you can repay your FFEL Loan. You can change the plan every year by contacting your lender. **Standard plan.** You pay a fixed amount every month and can take up to ten years to repay. The minimum payment is $50 or at least as much as the interest that has *accrued* since the loan began. **Graduated plan.** You begin by making small payments and gradually increase the payment amounts as your income increases. Take up to ten years to repay. **Income-sensitive plan.** This plan bases the amount of each payment on your annual income and the loan amount. Like the graduated plan, the income-sensitive plan allows you to pay small amounts when you're just starting out after college and increase the payment amounts as you can afford to do so. The minimum payment must be at least as much as the interest that has accrued since the loan began. You can take up to ten years to repay. **Extended plan.** If you have more than $30,000 in outstanding loans, this plan allows you to take up to 25 years to repay in full.

A TIME LIMIT ON CANCELLATIONS

Your college must notify you when it credits your account with Stafford Loan funds. You can tell the college you're cancelling all or a part of the loan if you do it within either 14 days of being notified or on the first day of the payment period, whichever is later. If the loan is paid to you directly, you can cancel it simply by not cashing the check.

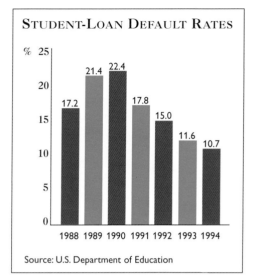

STUDENT-LOAN DEFAULT RATES

Source: U.S. Department of Education

KNOW YOUR RIGHTS AND RESPONSIBILITIES

RIGHTS

When applying for a loan, you must be told about:

- Any fees or charges;
- The interest rate, annual percentage rate (APR), and full amount of the loan;
- The repayment schedule, including when repayment begins;
- The effects of defaulting on your loan;
- Your options for consolidating and refinancing loans.

RESPONSIBILITIES

You should:

- Know the total amount you're eligible to borrow;
- Know your lender and how to contact him or her;
- Sign a note promising to repay the loan (whether or not the student graduates);
- Participate in loan counseling before receiving the first installment;
- Make payments on time even if you don't receive a bill.

CONSOLIDATE LOANS AND SIMPLIFY DEBT

*Y*ou may be able to combine some or all of your loans into a single consolidation loan from the U.S. Department of Education. Most federal loans and PLUS Loans may be consolidated. Consolidation loans are available through a participating bank or credit union.

RECEIVE ONE NEW INTEREST RATE

The interest rate on a FFEL Consolidation Loan is based on a calculation that combines all the loan amounts and their various interest rates. You may end up with a lower rate on the consolidated loan, but in some cases the rate could be higher than on one or more of your individual loans.

The Direct Consolidation Loan is different. The rate varies according to where interest rates in general are at the time. By law, though, the interest rate has never been higher than 9% on a Direct PLUS Consolidation Loan or higher than 8.25% on a Direct Subsidized or Unsubsidized Consolidation Loan.

29 If you default on your loan but meet certain conditions, you may be able to convert the loan to a Direct Consolidation Loan.

30 Consolidation is available for both subsidized and unsubsidized loans.

CHOOSE A PAYMENT PLAN

You can choose one of the following three payment plans with a federal loan:

Standard. This option lets you make equal payments monthly for 10 years;

Extended. Here, you make smaller monthly payments spread out over 15, 25, or 30 years;

Graduated. You also have the option to make monthly payments that gradually increase as your income increases.

YOU HAVE RIGHTS TO A LOAN

According to the U.S. Department of Education Financial Aid Student Guide, you may not be refused a consolidated loan because of the:

● Number or type of loans you have;
● School you attend;
● Interest rate you would be charged;
● Types of repayment schedules available to you.

31 Even if you have only one loan, you can get a Direct Consolidation Loan and receive benefits such as flexible payment options.

FOR MORE INFORMATION

For all the rules and procedures, you may contact the loan consolidation department of any participating lender (ask your financial aid office for referrals) or you can call the Loan Origination Center's Consolidation Department at 800-557-7392.

KNOW HOW MUCH DEBT YOU CAN CARRY

*H*ow will you know what you can afford to repay? Lenders make that assessment based on the following formula, which some use loosely and others consider a strict guideline.

HOUSING

+

No more than 28% of gross monthly income (the total amount, not just your take-home pay) should be going to pay for housing (mortgage and other home loans, or rent).

ALL OTHER RECURRING DEBT

=

No more than 9% of gross monthly income should be going toward all other loans such as student loans, car loans, credit cards, and similar loans.

TOTAL DEBT

No more than 37% of your gross monthly income should be going to pay loans each month. Some lenders will turn you down if you're above the 37% mark. If a lender grants the loan anyway, be aware that it will be a significant debt to carry.

LOAN REPAYMENT CHART

The amount listed in the total interest column is the amount you will pay in addition to the total amount borrowed.

INTEREST RATE		7.00%		8.25%		9.00%	
Total amount borrowed	No. of payments	Payment	Total interest	Payment	Total interest	Payment	Total interest
$3,000	76	$50	$720	$50	$850	$52	$933
$5,000	120	$58	$1,966	$61	$2,359	$63	$2,601
$8,000	120	$93	$3,147	$98	$3,774	$101	$4,161
$10,000	120	$116	$3,933	$123	$4,718	$127	$5,201
$16,000	120	$186	$6,292	$196	$7,549	$207	$8,322
$20,000	120	$232	$7,866	$245	$9,437	$253	$10,402
$25,000	120	$290	$9,832	$307	$11,796	$317	$13,003
$35,000	120	$406	$13,766	$429	$16,514	$443	$18,204
$50,000	120	$581	$19,666	$613	$23,591	$633	$26,006

Source: California Student Aid Commission Counselor's Guide, 2000-200C

ESTIMATED ENTRY LEVEL SALARIES
(PROJECTED IN 1999 FOR 2000)

POSITION	GROSS ANNUAL SALARY
Accountant	$29,400
Architect	$27,000
Chemist	$25,000
Assistant Professor	$40,100
Computer Programmer	$35,167
Computer Scientist and Systems Analyst	$36,597
Cosmetologist and Barber	$15,080
Dental Assistant	$18,772
Emergency/Medical Technician	$25.051
Engineer	$38,500
Firefighter	$34,216
Forestry/Conservation	$24,200
Graphic Designer	$23,000
Lawyer	$40,000
Librarian	$28,700
Mathematician	$31,800
Nurse	$36,244
Occupational Therapist	$40,560
Pharmacist	$51,584
Physical Therapist	$39,364
Police Officer	$34,700
Psychologist	$19,500
Secretary	$19,700
Travel Agent	$16,400
Veterinarian	$29,900

KEEP YOUR CREDIT RECORD CLEAN

Most financial aid offices check your credit before they will offer you aid. If the report shows a poor history, you may be denied aid. They may believe that you aren't responsible with money.

APPLYING FOR FINANCIAL AID

To receive financial aid from the federal government,
you must closely follow the rules for applying.

THE FAFSA IS YOUR ENTRYWAY

*T*he Free Application for Federal Student Aid (FAFSA) *is your key to entering the financial aid marketplace. It's used by the government to determine your EFC. It also automatically makes you eligible for most federal aid and many state and college-based aid. FAFSA is required by all financial aid offices. Some schools may also request a PROFILE application (see page 56). Here is an overview of the federal aid available when you file the FAFSA form.*

THINGS TO KNOW

You will need the following documents to complete the application process:

- Social Security card and drivers license;
- W-2 Forms or other income records;
- Your federal income tax return (and your spouse's, if you're married);
- Your parents' Federal Income Tax return
- Records of other untaxed income received such as welfare benefits, social security benefits, veterans benefits, or military or clergy allowances;
- Current bank statements and records of stocks, bonds, and other investments;
- Business or farm records, if applicable;
- Your alien registration card (if you are not a U.S. citizen).

32 Schools set their own deadlines for aid applications. Check with each school and do not miss their dates. There are no exceptions!

ENLIST FOR SERVICE

Every male applicant for federal financial aid must register with the Selective Service (the U.S. Armed Forces) upon turning 18 years of age. You can't receive aid unless you register.

Free Application for Federal Student Aid

OMB 1840-0610   July 1, 1999 — June 30, 2000 school year

Use this form to apply for federal student grants, work-study money, and loans.

You can also apply over the Internet at http://www.fafsa.ed.gov instead of using this paper form. In addition to federal student aid, you may also be eligible for a Hope or a Lifetime Learning income tax credit, both of which you claim when you file your taxes. For more information on these tax credits, this application, and the U.S. Department of Education's student aid programs, call 1-800-4FED-AID (1-800-433-3243) Monday through Friday between 8:00am and 8:00pm eastern time or look on the internet at http://www.ed.gov/offices/OPE. If you are hearing impaired, call TDD 1-800-730-8913.

Your answers on this form will be read by a machine. Therefore,

- use black ink or #2 pencil and fill in ovals completely, like this:
- print clearly in CAPITAL letters and skip a box between words: I S   E L M   S T
- report dollar amounts (such as $12,356.00) like this: $ 1 2 , 3 5 6 (no cents)
- write numbers less than 10 with a zero (0) first: 0 7

Yellow is for students and purple is for parents.

- If you are filing a **1998 income tax return**, we recommend that you fill it out before completing this form. However, you do not need to send your income tax return to the IRS before you fill out this form.
- After you complete this application, make a copy of it. Then **send the original of pages 3 through 6 in the attached envelope** and send it to Federal Student Aid Programs, P.O. Box 4008, Mt. Vernon, IL 62864-8608.
- Send in this application—pages 3 through 6—only between **January 1, 1999, and June 30, 2000**.
- You should hear from us within four weeks. If you do not, please call 1-319-337-5665.
- If you or your family has **unusual circumstances** (such as loss of employment or major medical expenses) that might affect your need for student financial aid, check with the financial aid office at the college you plan to attend.
- With this form you may also be able to apply for student aid from other sources, such as your state or college. The deadlines for states (see below) or colleges may be as early as January 1999, and you may be required to complete additional forms.

Now go to page 3 and begin filling out this form. Refer to the notes as needed.

Deadlines for state aid. Generally, state aid comes from your state of legal residence. Check with your high school guidance counselor or the financial aid administrator at your college about state and college sources of student financial aid. State deadlines are below.

◀ **FEDERAL AID**

This form opens the door to the following financial aid.

Free money. No repayment required:
- *Federal Pell Grant*
- *SEOG (Federal Supplemental Educational Opportunity Grant)*

Loans based on need (the government pays the interest while the student is in school):
- *Federal Perkins Loan*
- *Federal Family Education Loan (FFEL)*
- *Stafford Loan (subsidized version)*
- *Federal Ford Direct Loan*

Money the student earns:
- *Federal Work-Study Program*

Loans available regardless of need:
- *Stafford Loan (unsubsidized)*
- *PLUS Loan*

33 Apply as soon as you can after January 1. Don't date or send the FAFSA before then!

THE FAFSA PROCESS: TIMING IS CRUCIAL

T hese are the steps experts recommend that you follow to help assure a mistake-free FAFSA process.

1. OBTAIN AN APPLICATION

FAFSA is available in November or December from the high school guidance office. It's also available online at www.ed.gov/offices/OPE/express.html (to download the software needed to fill out the form).

2. REVIEW INSTRUCTIONS

The questionnaire itself is only four pages long, although the package looks bulky because of the lengthy instructions. The instructions, however, are simple and step-by-step, so the form also looks harder than it actually is. Completing **FAFSA** should take two or three hours; not bad if it means you will receive financial aid for up to four years of school. There's an addressed envelope, so you only have to add a stamp.

34 Call the Federal Student Aid Information Center at 800-4FEDAID if you need help.

8. CHECK THE SAR

Check the **SAR** for accuracy and correct errors immediately. The **SAR** will tell you how to report errors. It's wise to be as accurate and complete as possible the first time around. The time required to correct errors later will delay the application and could cause you to lose some aid.

7. RECEIVE A RESPONSE

About four to six weeks after submitting the **FAFSA**, you will receive a **Student Aid Report (SAR)**. If you don't get it by then, call to follow up. The **SAR** is the letter that shows your **EFC** and notifies you of your eligibility (or ineligibility) for federal aid programs. The **EFC** amount shown (which has no dollar sign, so don't be confused) is what your family will be expected to pay toward a year of school.

3. FILL OUT STUDENT INFORMATION

These are personal questions such as the educational background, future plans, the kind of college degree anticipated, and the types of financial aid the student hopes to receive.

4. FILL OUT PARENT INFORMATION

These are personal and financial questions. Many involve information from bank and brokerage statements. If the previous year's tax return hasn't been prepared yet, you should estimate annual income from pay stubs or other means. There are also questions about the household: who lives there and for how long, the family income and other earnings, and employee benefits, if any. It also asks about the family assets such as personal property and real estate.

Send to:
U.S. Department of Education

or

Complete online at:
www.fafsa.gov

5. LIST THE COLLEGES AND SIGN

You're asked to list six colleges you want your information to be sent to. Finally, both the student and a parent must sign the application. Remember to do this! Failure to sign **FAFSA** is the top reason for unprocessed and returned applications. List all the colleges you plan to apply to even if they're also on your **PROFILE** list (see page 56).

6. SEND IT EARLY

Forms are accepted only between January 1 and June 30. Many schools have limited funds. It's wise to mail the form on January 1 or very soon thereafter. Forms obtained online can be submitted online.

THE PROFILE PROCESS

A bout five hundred schools, typically private schools, require another application called PROFILE. It's a customized application created for you based on information you provide in a registration form. Be sure to call the financial aid offices of the schools you're considering to see whether they require PROFILE.

1. OBTAIN A REGISTRATION FORM

You can get the registration form in October or November in one of these ways:

- **You can receive the form from your high school guidance counselor or the college financial aid office;**
- **You can obtain and submit it at www.collegeboard.org or through the online service called EXPAN, which is available at participating high schools. Have a credit card number ready or ask to be billed;**
- **You can also register over the phone by calling 800-778-6888. Have a credit card ready or ask to be billed.**

2. LIST THE SCHOOLS

On the form, list only the schools that you want to receive your customized PROFILE application.

WHY SCHOOLS WANT IT

In determining financial need, FAFSA excludes the value of certain assets such as home equity and retirement plan savings. Many colleges have their own funds to disburse according to their own standards and want a fuller picture of your financial need. PROFILE, therefore, takes a closer look at family finances and may lead to a higher EFC than you will get from FAFSA.

3. PAY A SERVICE FEE

PROFILE is a service run by the College Scholarship Service (CSS) in Princeton, NJ. They charge about $20 for each school you list. A fee waiver may be possible for at least one school. Check with your guidance counselor. If there isn't a check or credit card number enclosed, your form will be returned unprocessed. CSS suggests you send it by regular mail. Any "special handling" may delay processing.

7. COLLEGES RECEIVE INFORMATION

Each college on your list receives a customized application. They then use it to estimate your eligibility for aid, although it isn't binding. For instance, a college cannot offer federal financial aid without receiving the results from the **FAFSA**. A college may also ask for income tax records, bank and investment account statements, or other documents to verify finances. Reply quickly.

6. CSS SENDS A RESPONSE

You should receive a package from **CSS** within a few weeks. Call if you don't receive it. The package includes:
- A receipt that you've registered and the list of schools that will receive the application;
- An Additional School Request section in case you want to add schools not listed when you first mailed in the form;
- Any additional forms a college may want you to complete.
  If you paid for it, there will also be a **Data Confirmation** section with a record of the family information you provided. Check for accuracy and follow instructions for correcting errors immediately.

Request online at:
http://profileonline.cbreston.org

or

Call 1-800-239-5888

5. COMPLETE THE CUSTOMIZED APPLICATION

CSS will send you an application customized with the questions your schools specifically want answered. Be as accurate and complete as possible. The time required to correct inaccuracies later will delay the application and could cause you to lose some aid.

4. PAY MORE FOR MORE SERVICES

You can pay an additional fee to order a **Data Confirmation Report** at the time you register. This report gives you an opportunity to catch errors and verify that your application will be sent to the correct schools.

35 A PROFILE is required for some scholarships, including the National Merit Scholarship.

YOU RECEIVE THE SAR

*T*he Student Aid Report (SAR) acknowledges receipt of FAFSA and confirms its information. The SAR is several pages long, broken into three parts. Review it carefully. The financial aid officers will use this document as your official record in determining your aid package. These pages show two key parts of the SAR.

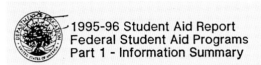

1995-96 Student Aid Report
Federal Student Aid Programs
Part 1 - Information Summary

CCCCC
OMB No. 1840-0132
Form Approved
Exp. 12-31-96

*0025*70 *866*

IMPORTANT: Read ALL information in Part 1 to find out what to do with this Report.

003094C064

April 17, 1995
Page 1 of 5
EFC: 00825*

Read this letter carefully and review each item on Part 2 of this Student Aid Report (SAR). Follow the instructions at the top of Part 2 and in the Free Application for Federal Student Aid (FAFSA) instruction booklet to help you make corrections. For additional help with your SAR, contact your Financial Aid Administrator (FAA).

If all the information on this SAR is correct, you may be eligible to receive a Federal Pell Grant and other Federal student aid in 1995-96. Your FAA will determine whether you meet all eligibility requirements to receive aid. The amount of aid will depend on the cost of attendance at your school, your enrollment status (full-time, three-quarter-time, half-time, or less than half-time), Congressional budget rest ti ar ors.

▲ **PART 1:**
INFORMATION SUMMARY
This section summarizes the information you provided. After your first year of college, the SAR will also show your financial aid history. The most important part of the summary is your EFC in the upper right. Your financial aid potential is highly dependent on this figure. Be sure it is correct. For 2000-2001, any number under 2926 is eligible for a Pell Grant. The lower the number, the more financial aid you may receive.

36 The SAR shows your EFC and lets you know whether you are eligible for the Pell Grant and other forms of aid.

▼ PART 2:
INFORMATION REVIEW

This section lists all the details of the information you provided on the FAFSA. To the right of the information are boxes for you to enter corrections. As always, correct errors immediately. There may be assumptions made in this section (marked "assumed") based on information you provided. Check these carefully.

37 Lying on the FAFSA is against the law. You could go to jail or have to pay a fine.

This section contains information from your student aid application (shaded items display parents' information, i... Information Review Form (Part 2 of your SAR) to correct this information. **Do not make corrections on thi**

1. LAST NAME	
2. FIRST NAME	
3. MIDDLE INITIAL	F
5. CITY	
6. STATE ABBREVIATION	
7. ZIP CODE	
8. SOCIAL SECURITY NUMBER	
9. DATE OF BIRTH	
10. PERMANENT HOME PHONE NUMBER	
11. STATE OF LEGAL RESIDENCE	
12. DATE YOU BECAME A LEGAL RESIDENT	
13. DRIVER'S LICENSE STATE ABBREVIATION	
14. DRIVER'S LICENSE NUMBER	
15. CITIZENSHIP STATUS	U.S. CITIZEN
16. ALIEN REGISTRATION NUMBER	
17. MARITAL STATUS	UNMARRIED
18. DATE OF MARITAL STATUS	(BLANK)
19. FIRST BACHELOR'S DEGREE BY 7-1-95?	NO
20. HIGH SCHOOL GRADUATION DATE	JUNE 1995
21. GED DIPLOMA DATE	(BLANK)
22. FATHER'S EDUCATIONAL LEVEL	COLLEGE
23. MOTHER'S EDUCATIONAL LEVEL	COLLEGE
24. ENROLLMENT STATUS SUMMER TERM 1995	(BLANK)
25. ENROLLMENT STATUS FALL SEM/QTR 1995	FULL TIME
26. ENROLLMENT STATUS WINTER QTR 1995-96	FULL TIME
27. ENROLLMENT STATUS SPRING SEM/QTR 1996	FULL TIME
28. ENROLLMENT STATUS SUMMER TERM 1996	FULL TIME
29. COURSE OF STUDY	BIOSCIENCE
30. TYPE OF DEGREE/CERTIFICATE	1ST BA
31. DATE EXPECT TO RECEIVE DEGREE	JUNE 01, 1999
32. GRADE LEVEL IN COLLEGE IN 1995-96	1ST NEVER ATTENDED
33. INTERESTED IN EMPLOYMENT?	(BLANK)
34. INTERESTED IN STUDENT LOANS?	(BLANK)
35. INTERESTED IN PARENT LOANS?	(BLANK)
36. ATTENDING SAME COLLEGE IN 1995?	(BLANK)
37. WILL PAY DEPENDENT CARE FOR HOW MANY?	
38. MONTHLY VA BENEFITS AMOUNT	$
39. HOW MANY MONTHS RECEIVING VA BENEFITS?	
40. BORN BEFORE 1-1-72?	NO
41. VETERAN OF U.S. ARMED FORCES?	NO
42. ENROLLED IN GRADUATE PROGRAM 1995-96?	NO
43. ARE YOU MARRIED?	NO
44. ORPHAN OR WARD OF COURT?	NO
45. HAVE DEPENDENTS OTHER THAN SPOUSE?	NO
46. NUMBER OF FAMILY MEMBERS IN 1995-96	DO NOT CORRECT
47. NUMBER IN COLLEGE IN 1995-96	DO NOT CORRECT
48. MARITAL STATUS	(BLANK)
49. STATE OF LEGAL RESIDENCE	CA
50. DATE PARENT(S) BECAME LEGAL RESIDENTS	JUNE 22, 1987
51. NUMBER OF FAMILY MEMBERS IN 1995-96	04
52. NUMBER IN COLLEGE IN 1995-96	2

53. TYPE OF 1994 TAX FORM USED	
54. EXEMPTIONS CLAIMED	
55. ADJUSTED GROSS INCOME FROM IRS FORM	
56. U.S. INCOME TAX PAID	
57. STUDENT'S INCOME EARNED FROM WORK	
58. SPOUSE'S INCOME EARNED FROM WORK	
59. ANNUAL SOCIAL SECURITY BENEFITS	
60. ANNUAL AFDC/ADC	
61. ANNUAL CHILD SUPPORT RECEIVED	
62. OTHER UNTAXED INCOME	
63. 1994 EXCLUSIONS, WORKSHEET #3	
64. TYPE OF 1994 TAX FORM USED	
65. EXEMPTIONS CLAIMED	
66. ADJUSTED GROSS INCOME FROM IRS FORM	
67. U.S. INCOME TAX PAID	
68. FATHER'S INCOME EARNED FROM WORK	
69. MOTHER'S INCOME EARNED FROM WORK	
70. ANNUAL SOCIAL SECURITY BENEFITS	
71. ANNUAL AFDC/ADC	
72. ANNUAL CHILD SUPPORT RECEIVED	
73. OTHER UNTAXED INCOME	
74. 1994 EXCLUSIONS, WORKSHEET #3	
75. CASH, SAVINGS, AND CHECKING	
76. OTHER REAL ESTATE/INVESTMENT VALUE	
77. OTHER REAL ESTATE/INVESTMENT DEBT	
78. BUSINESS VALUE	
79. BUSINESS DEBT	
80. FARM VALUE	
81. FARM DEBT	
82. AGE OF OLDER PARENT	
83. CASH, SAVINGS, AND CHECKING	
84. OTHER REAL ESTATE/INVESTMENT VALUE	
85. OTHER REAL ESTATE/INVESTMENT DEBT	
86. BUSINESS VALUE	
87. BUSINESS DEBT	
88. FARM VALUE	
89. FARM DEBT	
90. FIRST COLLEGE NAME	UNIVERSIT
91. FIRST HOUSING STATUS	CAMPUS
92. SECOND COLLEGE NAME	UNIVERSI
93. SECOND HOUSING STATUS	CAMPUS
94. THIRD COLLEGE NAME	UNIVERSI
95. THIRD HOUSING STATUS	CAMPUS
96. FOURTH COLLEGE NAME	
97. FOURTH HOUSING STATUS	(BLANK)
98. FIFTH COLLEGE NAME	
99. FIFTH HOUSING STATUS	(BLANK)
100. SIXTH COLLEGE NAME	
101. SIXTH HOUSING STATUS	(BLANK)
102. SHOULD DATA BE RELEASED TO STATE?	
103. REGISTER YOU FOR SELECTIVE SERVIC	
104. SIGNED BY?	
105. DATE COMPLETED	
106. PREPARER'S EIN	
107. PREPARER'S SOCIAL SECURITY NUMBER	
108. PREPARER'S SIGNATURE	

Student's Use Box   EFC: 00825*   SEC. EFC:

CERTIFICATION STATEMENT ON REFUNDS AND DEFAULT

I certify that I do not owe a refund on any grant or loan, am not in default on any loan or have made satisfactory arrangements to repay any defaulted loan, and have not borrowed in excess of the loan limits, under Title IV programs, at any institution.

STATEMENT OF EDUCATIONAL PURPOSE

I will use all Title IV money received only for expenses related to my study at

UNIVERSITY OF CALIFORNIA LOS ANGELES
(Name of Institution)

STATEMENT OF REGISTRATION S

____ I certify that I am registered wit

__X__ I certify that I am not required t Selective Service because

____ I am a female
____ I am in the armed servi... not apply to members of Guard who are not on ac
____ I have not reached my 1
__X__ I was born before 1960
____ I am a resident of the F or the Marshall Islands, the Trust Territory of t

THINGS TO KNOW

THINGS TO KNOW

● If your EFC has an asterisk next to it, you're one of approximately 30% of applicants chosen at random by the U.S. Department of Education to verify your information. You will be asked to supply proof of financial status, family size, and possibly of citizenship or other eligibility requirements.

● Fill out the verification worksheet and send with the other documents to the college financial aid office. The information you send is verified by the colleges, the state, or the U.S. Department of Education. If it's discovered that you have received aid falsely, you will have to repay it.

THE AWARD LETTER

*I*f you're admitted to a school and offered financial aid, you will receive an award letter describing the financial aid package—the exact types and amounts of aid being offered. Remember, colleges have goals, too. They want to invest their money in students who not only have the potential to achieve their own goals but the school's goals as well.

OUTSIDE AID

If a school is going to reduce aid because you've received outside aid, they will usually reduce the loans before reducing grants and scholarships.

The Aid Package
This is the total aid offered. Colleges often try to balance grants and scholarships with loans so you won't have a large debt burden after graduating. Assistance packages will vary, even among schools with similar COAs, because financial aid officers use their past experiences to interpret your situation. Each college has its own formula for mixing types of aid.

UNIVERSITY OF CALIFORNIA, LOS ANGELES

BERKELEY · DAVIS · IRVINE · LOS ANGELES · RIVERSIDE · SAN DIEGO · SAN FRA

1999-00 ACADEMIC YEAR
FINANCIAL AID NOTIFICATI

AWARD NAME	FALL	WINTER	SPRI
CAL GRANT A	1,143.00	1,143.00	1,14
FEDERAL PELL GRANT	958.34	958.33	95
FED SUBSIDIZED STAFFORD LOAN	1,833.34	1,833.33	1,83
FEDERAL PARENT LOAN (PLUS)	516.68	516.66	51
TOTAL ALL FUNDS	4,451.36	4,451.32	4,45

YOU HAVE THREE CHOICES

Ask for more money (appeal). If your circumstances have changed since you applied, you can ask to have your package reviewed. Be sure to have proof of your claims. Be aware that negotiating or badgering may turn off the financial aid officer. Stating your case as a request will probably be treated with respect.

Accept some aid, decline some. You can turn down part of an award, such as the loan or work-study. You will be asked to sign off on each individual offer.

Look further to fill the gap. You can find other sources for loans and/or jobs, or you can use more of your own money.

The COA
This number is the estimated cost to attend a year at this school (a number you should already know by the time you apply).

Your EFC
Deduct the amount your family is expected to contribute (the EFC calculated from FAFSA).

The Unmet Need
Remember the formula on pages 6-7? This is where you see it in reality. If your EFC and financial aid do not cover the entire COA, you're left with "unmet need." This may be because the school lacks funds, other students have more pressing needs, or you are not a high-priority student for that school.

UCLA

SANTA BARBARA · SANTA CRUZ

FINANCIAL AID OFFICE
BOX 951435
A129-J MURPHY HALL
LOS ANGELES, CA 90095-1435

(310) 206-0400
August 25, 1999
SECOND NOTICE

GRAD RES OFF-CAMPUS
13,578.00
0.00 Parent Contribution
224.00 Student Contribution
13,354.00 Financial Need

AL	ACCEPT	DECLINE
29.00	A	D
75.00	A	D
00.00	A	D
50.00	A	D
64.00		

38 Like most of us, schools have limited financial resources to meet their goals.

COMPARE PACKAGES

Compare at least the following elements in each aid package you receive.

Needs met. The first test is to see which college comes closest to meeting your total financing needs (this should not be the only determining factor).

Ratio of grants to loans. Compare the free money versus the loans offered in each college's package. You may find that a more expensive college is offering a package that will leave you with less debt than you would have from a less expensive college.

Loans. A smaller loan may have a higher interest rate than the larger loan and actually cost more.

Renewability. Make sure the aid components are renewable.

Award reductions. Find out whether any outside aid will cause the school to reduce your package—and if so, what part it will reduce.

BE PREPARED AS YOU GO

*Y*ou can help your chances of affording college if you start
planning early. Student and parent should work as a team
on two fronts. First, the financial front: find ways to save money
and invest it wisely. Second, the personal front: develop strong
study habits, get good grades, and be involved in worthwhile
activities. These tasks increase the chances of acceptance, and
they may influence the amount of financial aid you're offered.
Here are some steps to take while in high school.

FRESHMAN YEAR
- Get Social Security number if you don't have one.
- Ask guidance counselor to help design a curriculum
  of college-bound courses, and find scholarships lists.
- Start college savings account and work part-time jobs.
- Begin exploring websites for information on financial aid.
  Update every year.
- Parent: Begin shifting savings to more stable, predictable
  types of investments.

Spring/Summer
- Practice taking PSAT and ACT.
- Create resume of extracurricular activities. Keep updated.

SOPHOMORE YEAR
- If thinking of military academy, contact congressional
  representative to discuss your nomination. For other military
  assistance, contact local recruiting office.
- Consider part-time, summer, or volunteer activity related
  to your interests.
- Talk to guidance counselor and older students about
  upcoming SAT and ACT exams.

Spring/Summer
- Contact state guaranty agency for information on financial aid.
- Start ordering college catalogs.
- Begin working on college application essay.

JUNIOR YEAR

- In October, take PSAT/ NMSQT test for National Merit Scholarship.
- Participate in school or community workshops related to financial aid.
- Visit colleges of interest and meet with admissions and financial aid officers.
- Review high school course selections with guidance counselor to see if you're still on track.
- Take SAT or ACT.
- Find out if schools on your list offer early admission. Note deadlines.
- In January: Family income during this calendar year is used to determine your financial need, whether or not you qualify for federal financial aid.

Spring

- Review test scores with guidance counselor. Retake tests, if necessary.
- Begin narrowing list of schools.
- Take any tests required by schools.

Summer

- Narrow scholarship and grant search.
- Military academy applicants: give congressional representative all requested information.

 39 If you can't afford the exam fees, ask your guidance counselor about fee waivers.

SENIOR YEAR

- Meet with guidance counselor to be sure you will meet all admission requirements at each school.
- Submit early admission applications on time. Keep copies.
- Get federal aid applications from a guidance counselor (usually in October or November).
- Complete all applications for schools and financial aid, and submit them before the deadlines. Keep copies.
- As soon as possible after January 1, submit the FAFSA. Electronic filing is quickest. You will receive the SAR that scores your financial need about six weeks later.
- Contact state guaranty agency for financial aid opportunities.
- Investigate tuition payment options at each school.
- Register with the military upon turning 18 (males only).

Spring

- Write a letter of acceptance to the school of your choice and notify any other schools of your decision.
- Sign your award letter, make copies, and return the original to the financial aid office of your college.
- Notify the financial aid office of any awards or scholarships you receive from other sources.
- Complete loan applications if you're trying to raise additional funding.
- Contact financial aid office if there have been any significant changes in finances since you applied.

DIFFERENT SCHOOLS, DIFFERENT OPPORTUNITIES

*I*t's important not to think of colleges in general terms. There are many choices among schools. Some offer a variety of ways to save time or money. Others offer a wide variety of ways to learn. It may be easier than you think to find a college, because schools have been created specifically to meet people's varying needs.

FOUR-YEAR COLLEGE

- Offers Bachelor of Science (B.S.) or Arts (B.A.) degree;
- Offers no graduate programs;
- Has on-campus housing.

FOUR-YEAR UNIVERSITY

- Offers Bachelor of Science (B.S.) or Arts (B.A.) degree;
- Typically has a larger student population;
- Offers graduate programs;
- Has on-campus housing.

TECHNICAL SCHOOL

- Offers a hands-on education;
- Runs as a for-profit business;
- Typically is more expensive than state schools, less expensive than private schools;
- May not offer housing;
- Some offer two-year degrees others four-year degrees;
- Must be accredited (many aren't) and participate in federal financial aid programs (if you want federal financial aid).

QUESTIONS FOR PROSPECTIVE COLLEGES

- How many students study in your field of interest?
- How many students get jobs in their field of interest?
- What are the job placement rates, (especially for people interested in vocational programs)?

- What is the school's job placement service/career counseling?
- How many students who start at the school earn a certificate or degree?
- How many drop out? A high drop-out rate may indicate student dissatisfaction;
- How many go on to advanced degrees?

COMMUNITY COLLEGE

- Offers two-year associate degrees: an Associate of Arts (A.A.), Associate of Science (A.S.), and an Associate of Applied Science (A.A.S.);
- Public schools, designed to serve community residents;
- Cost per course credit is usually cheaper than at four-year schools;
- Tuition fees typically are lowest for local residents;
- May not require a high school diploma;
- On-campus housing is unlikely.

JUNIOR COLLEGE

- Offers two-year associate degrees: an Associate of Arts (A.A.), Associate of Science (A.S.), and an Associate of Applied Science (A.A.S.);
- Typically are private schools. Some train you for immediate employment, others prepare you to transfer to a four-year school to complete your bachelor's degree;
- Cost per course credit is usually cheaper than at four-year schools;
- Tuition fees are typically the same for all state residents;
- May not require a high school diploma;
- On-campus housing is unusual.

ACCREDITATION

If you're hoping for financial aid, be sure the schools are accredited by an agency recognized by the Secretary of Education and are eligible to participate in federal student aid programs. For more details, call 800-4FEDAID.

PEOPLE AND PLACES TO KNOW

It's helpful to know the roles of the players in the game. Here are some of them.

GUIDANCE COUNSELORS

Every high school has them. Some are more knowledgeable than others. Some have lists of scholarships and grants you might want, and most have copies of the FAFSA and PROFILE applications. Some have the resources to file your FAFSA electronically.

COLLEGE ADMISSIONS OFFICERS

The admissions officers are the ones who decide whether or not to accept you as a student. They will answer your questions and offer advice as you go through the admissions process. An admissions officer's main responsibility is to help the school achieve its admissions goals, which for example, may be to boost the quality of a program or department.

COLLEGE REPRESENTATIVES

These people are the college's ambassadors (recruiters) who visit high schools and talk about their school to students and parents.

COLLEGE FINANCIAL AID OFFICERS

These are on-campus advisors and assemblers of financial aid packages, the ones who decide which students receive what aid. These are the people to contact to learn as much as you can before applying.

THE COLLEGE BOARD

A non-profit association of more than 2,800 colleges and universities, this institution provides information on the PSAT/NMSQT and the SATs. They also sponsor the College-Level Examination Program (CLEP).

SALLIE MAE

Otherwise known as the Student Loan Marketing Association, this is a publicly traded company in the business of lending money for education loans (Stafford, PLUS, or private). For more information, call 800-892-5321. Their website is www.salliemae.com.

NELLIE MAE

This is the largest non-profit provider of education loans. They loan money to people whether or not they qualify for federal aid. To find out more, call 800-9-TUITION. Their website is www.nelliemae.org.

FEDERAL STUDENT AID INFORMATION CENTER

For help in obtaining FAFSA results (your financial need score), you may call this center at 319-337-5665. They can help you interpret your SAR (Student Aid Report) and get you a duplicate if necessary. Counselors at this number can assist you in completing the FAFSA and SAR, tell you a school's student loan default rate, and which schools participate in federal student aid programs. They can also explain federal aid eligibility requirements, the process of awarding aid, send you publications, tell you if your federal student financial aid application has been processed, and have your application information sent to a specific school. You can even notify them to forward a change in your address to the schools.

STATE GUARANTY AGENCY

Every state has one. It acts as an agent of the federal government to insure student loans so that if you default on your loan, the lender won't lose the money. It also administers its own state's aid programs. Staff members can answer questions about an existing loan or the state's scholarship and grant programs.

WEBSITES TO KNOW

College opportunities online
www.ed.gov/prog/ipeds/cool
FAFSA on the web
www.fafsa.ed.gov
Helping complete the FAFSA
www.ed.gov/prog_info/SFA/FAFSA
Fastweb
www.fastweb.com
Occupational Outlook Handbook
www.bls.gov/ocohome.htm
Employment trends
www.edd.cahwnet.gov

FINANCIAL AID AT A GLANCE

Action	Pell Grant	SEOG Grant	Perkins Loan
Who may apply	All full- and half-time students in a degree program U.S. citizens or eligible noncitizens	All full- and half-time students in a degree program U.S. citizens or eligible noncitizens	All full- and half-time students in a degree program U.S. citizens or eligible noncitizens
How to apply	File FAFSA	File FAFSA Based on fund availability	File FAFSA Based on fund availability
How awards are determined	Based on financial need	Based on financial need	Based on financial need
Award amounts	(Changes each year) Maximum: $3,125 Minimum: $400	Depends on financial need and other aid received	Depends on financial need and other aid received 5% interest, repayment begins nine months after graduation
Priority filing deadline	FAFSA must be filed by May 1	FAFSA must be filed by March 2	FAFSA must be filed by March 2

Subsidized Stafford Loan	Unsubsidized Stafford Loan	PLUS Loan	Federal Work-Study Program
All full- and half-time students in a degree program U.S. citizens or eligible noncitizens	All full- and half-time students in a degree program U.S. citizens or eligible noncitizens	All parents of full- and half-time students in a degree program U.S. citizens or eligible noncitizens	All full- and half-time students in a degree program U.S. citizens or eligible noncitizens
File FAFSA	File FAFSA	File FAFSA	File FAFSA
Based on financial need and grade level	Determined by student based upon Financial Aid Office recommendation	Determined by parent based upon Financial Aid Office recommendation	Based on financial need and funds availability
Maximum annual limits: Freshman: $2,625 Sophomore: $3,500 Juniors and Seniors: $5,500	Combined subsidized and unsubsidized amount for dependent students: Freshman: $2,625 Sophomore: $3,500 Junior/Senior: $5,500 or independent students: Freshman: $6,625 Sophomore: $7,500 Junior/Senior: $10,500	Maximum can't exceed the student's COA minus other aid received	Depends on financial need Maximum: $1,800 If employed by approved community service agency, can petition to have award increased to $5,000
FAFSA must be filed by May 1 (subject to the school's own deadlines)	FAFSA must be filed by May 1 (subject to the school's own deadlines)	FAFSA must be filed by May 1 (subject to the school's own deadlines)	FAFSA must be filed by March 2

INDEX

ACKNOWLEDGMENTS

AUTHORS' ACKNOWLEDGMENTS

The production of this book has called on the skills of many people. We would like particularly to mention our editors at Dorling Kindersley, and our consultant, Nick Clemente. Marc wishes to dedicate this book to Zachary Robinson for his great patience and support when it was most needed. Ronald wishes to dedicate this book to his courageous and loving wife, Barbara, his family and many cherished friends, and the many educators who work unselfishly to make educational opportunity a reality for all.

PUBLISHER'S ACKNOWLEDGMENTS

Dorling Kindersley would like to thank everyone who generously lent props for the photo shoots, and the following for their help and participation:

Editorial Ruth Strother; Stephanie Rubenstein; **Design and layout** Hedayat Sandjari; **Preflighting** Mark Schroeder **Consultants** Nick Clemente; Skeeter; **Indexer** Rachel Rice; **Proofreader** Stephanie Rubenstein; **Photography** Anthony Nex; **Photographers' assistants** Victor Boghassian; Stephanie Fowler; **Models** Stephanie Fowler; Griffin Nex; **Picture researcher** Mark Dennis; Sam Ruston; **Additional photo credits:** Rifle, page 35, David Edge; Key, page 18, Science Museum; Dolls, pages 30, 31, Wenham Museum, Wenhma, MA, and Faith Eaton.

Special thanks to Teresa Clavasquin for her generous support and assistance.

AUTHORS' BIOGRAPHIES

Ronald W. Johnson has been Director of Financial Aid at UCLA since 1995. Recognized nationally as an expert in his field, he has served on the executive boards of state, regional, and national educational associations and has spoken at numerous educational conferences throughout the country. Previously, he was Director of Financial Aid at Golden Gate University in San Francisco (1971-1974), Assistant Director in Charge of Counseling and Opportunity Programs (1974-1980), and then Director of Financial Aid (1980-1995) at the University of California-Davis. Ron also serves on numerous local, state, regional, and national Advisory Boards. His 31-year commitment to Student Financial Aid Administration has been acknowledged through many awards for his distinguished accomplishment and service to all students.

Marc Robinson is co-founder of Internet-based moneytours.com, a personal finance resource for corporations, universities, credit unions, and other institutions interested in helping their constituents make intelligent decisions about their financial lives. He wrote the original *The Wall Street Journal Guide to Understanding Money and Markets*, created *The Wall Street Journal Guide to Understanding Personal Finance*, co-published a series with Time Life Books, and wrote a children's book about onomateopia in different languages. In his two decades in the financial services industry, Marc has provided marketing consulting to many top Wall Street firms. He is admitted to practice law in New York State.